CW00923557

The Eternal Word,
the One God, the Free Spirit,
speaks through Gabriele,
as through all the prophets of God—
Abraham, Job, Moses, Elijah, Isaiah,
Jesus of Nazareth,
the Christ of God

Inner Prayer

Heart Prayer
Soul Prayer
Ether Prayer
Healing Prayer

by Gabriele

Gabriele
Publishing House

"Inner Prayer"

Third Edition, July 2024
© Gabriele-Verlag Das Wort GmbH
Max-Braun-Str. 2, 97828 Marktheidenfeld, Germany
www.gabriele-verlag.com
www.gabriele-publishing-house.com

Translated from the original German title:

„Inneres Beten"

The German edition is the work of reference
for all questions regarding the meaning of the contents.

Order No. S307MIEN

All decorative letters: © Gabriele-Verlag Das Wort

Printed by:
KlarDruck GmbH, Marktheidenfeld, Germany

ISBN 978-3-96446-577-1

Contents

Preface

Ever more people, especially the younger generation, are searching and asking for the meaning of life. They are looking for a meaningful existence and can find it only with difficulty. Many are weary of a life of prosperity; it is no longer able to satisfy them. They suffer from material abundance, from the push and pressure of wanting to be and to have. In view of the many threatening developments and alarming escalations, they increasingly sense that all living conditions are endangered.

Therefore, many of our fellow brothers and sisters are seeking the truth. Their inner unease, their searching and striving, is deep-rooted:

The soul, which is not of this world, senses its eternal homeland, where there is secureness and safety. It senses its connection with heavenly beings, among whom happiness, contentment, harmony and love prevail. Without the person being aware of it, the searching soul also longs for the dual unity, for its dual partner, who may live far from this Earth in the light-filled spheres of the eternal homeland. Soul and person are continuously on a journey. Unswervingly, the wayfarer strives for new goals that promise fulfillment. Once these goals have been reached, however, there is but a brief rest; fulfillment and satisfaction are of short duration. Nowhere can soul and person find the deep secureness, nowhere the lasting home.

The awakened soul feels that it is merely on a journey. It feels and senses higher things. This pressing sensation and longing of the soul awaken the person. The person who is awakening to spirituality begins to search for what is higher, nobler and more perfect. The efforts of the soul, which is striving toward its origin, communicates itself to its human being. It penetrates him and rises up in him like the revitalizing sap in a tree as springtime draws near.

The awakened soul already hears the calling of the Spirit. Caringly and lovingly, the Spirit encourages the soul like a mother bird that tries to stir her fledgling to leave its nest and learn to fly. "Come," she encourages. "Come and use your wings. Soar into the element, which is your life! Experience the freedom and vastness that is your home!" In the same way, the Spirit calls and encourages the awakened soul to climb higher, to enter the eternal life, which is its own.

The person does indeed sense the longing urge of his soul. The call of the Spirit, "Come follow Me," builds up more and more in his consciousness. However, the light of the inner being is not yet able to fully penetrate the veil of haze of this human side of life. The primordial melody of life is not yet able to prevail over the loud din of the worldly. The intellect still overlies the spiritual sensations, the quiet voice of the eternal truth.

A person turns here and there to find what his heart is so restlessly seeking and has to realize that it cannot be found externally. But where is there room for a spiritual life in the hustle and bustle, in the rush and rest-lessness of our fast-paced times?

Possessions, prestige and pleasure are the standards of an affluent society. They characterize the thinking and acting of people today. Since such an orientation is contrary to a spiritual life, many people believe that a spiritual life is closed to the one who stands in this world.

Through our occupational and social entanglements, we are all connected with the life of this world. This external life claims and burdens us more than ever. People are unable to free themselves from it. Technology offers us diverse and ever new possibilities: sensual stimulations and sounds, fascinations and distractions of all kinds, which often exceed the individual's capacity to understand. The tranquility and internalization that the soul calls for, therefore, seem like a utopia to many, for the realization of which our restless world leaves no room.

However, this seems so only to those who think that one has to withdraw from the noisy hustle and bustle, from society and their occupation, in order to attain tranquility.

It is true that the hustle and bustle of this world has fascinated many and holds them captive. Admittedly, worldly people are bound by what they think and strive for. This is the case today, as it has been at all times. However, the renewal of a person from within, through a return to the forces inherent in him, is just as possible today as it has been at all times.

We do not have to withdraw from our daily life, from our occupation and from society in order to find tranquility in ourselves. We merely have to realize what is important:

To live *in* this world, but not to be *with* this world.

It depends on which forces we allow to govern us. It depends on which forces we allow to dominate us and our lives. If we orient ourselves to the world, the material, then the world, everything external, will have an influence on us. Then we are children of the world and share in all that is inherent in the external world. Although the spiritual reality is just as present, it cannot effectively support, inspire and guide us, because we have not turned to it. We have not consciously made a connection to it and have not reached out to it.

When we turn to the spiritual, the external world with its manifestations loses its influence. Although it is still there, it can no longer exert its power over us because we have reached out to the divine in us. We are now nourished, guided and governed by Him. We may now rest in Him.

Once we have gained a foothold in the spiritual life that is in us, the eternal Being is the firm ground on which we stand. Firmly rooted in this ground and trusting in the powers that flow to us from there, we can grow from it into the external life, in word and deed. The storms of time may indeed batter us, but ultimately, they cannot harm us, because we receive strength and resilience from the primordial basis of the eternal Being. Thus, we may rest in the spiritual, while fulfilling our tasks in the world.

Humankind's progressive spiritual ignorance has led many people to think that the material and the spiritual, the religious, are two spheres that are far removed from one another.

In reality, the coarse-material, the material spheres of being here on Earth are closely connected with the fine-material, spiritual realms. They are planes of vibration existing side by side and simultaneously. They permeate each other: Despite their different frequencies, the presence of one reality does not exclude the presence of the other—similarly as light and sound can be present in a room at the same time.

For this reason, we can indeed live in this world without, however, being with this world. We merely have to decide to give priority to the inner reality of all Being, to the divine. The one who is not with this world but merely lives in this world will place what is higher and more refined above what is base, above materialism, thus finding the way to inner tranquility. But those who live in this world and orient themselves to this world, that is, who are with this world, will not have their hearts filled with inner peace, because this world does not know the peace that flows from the deep source of divine power.

The connection between the material and the spiritual planes of Being is established through devotion. When we turn to the forces of eternal life, an uninterrupted stream of power flows, because God, our Father, never closes His source of primordial power to us.

Prayer is devotion. Those who pray close the circle of life. Those who pray in the right way each day, from their

19

heart, will maintain the inner peace even in the greatest uproar.

There is much spiritual knowledge in this world, but little actualization and even less fulfillment of the heart and soul!

The knowing person recognizes that in our time the primordial powers of life radiate increasingly into the souls of people so as to awaken them to spirituality. Thus, some people are awakening to the realization of the powerlessness and instability of external values and external existence. Many are no longer satisfied with possessing and representing something. The bread of the external, of the material, no longer satisfies many, and they recognize that the external values merely distract and scatter, offering no substance for their life. All too often they prove to be hollow, stale and ephemeral. They impoverish the heart and bring no stillness or peace.

Where can the soul and person find the bread of life? Wherever we search, with friends, in this or that place, at external festivities or meetings, we do not find it—when it is not in us, in our inner being.

Many are driven, for the awakened soul urges them; however, they still search where they cannot find, and become numb in this world. They are unable to perceive what is so near to them! And when they hear of it, this often does not help them, because the intellect, the mind that is oriented toward material reality, still rejects and discards.

Yet, the forces from the highly vibrating cosmic spheres strive unceasingly to awaken and vivify. Their activity on our planet can be recognized everywhere and in many forms, for the Spirit of God works in manifold ways to bring home to many people an awareness of their spiritual origin, which especially at this time opens the way to the universal life. Each of us is guided in such a way that we are given the opportunity several times during our life on Earth to recognize what is needed: To recognize that we belong to the eternal, spiritual Being and that it is imperative to again seek and develop this origin in ourselves.

The day when a person realizes who he truly is, the day when a person finds himself is of decisive significance for his life, a life that does not end with the termination of this sojourn on Earth. It is the day on which he consciously turns to the eternal spiritual life. The person realizes that tranquility, contentment and the forces of infinite fullness, which he may open up through the divine All-love, are effective only in him, in his inner being.

Our Father, the eternal Spirit, has placed in each soul everything that He, the life, has brought forth and continuously brings forth as power and abundance. This fullness of spiritual power is more or less dormant in us. It wants to be awakened by us. However, if we want to attain inner peace and deep stillness, we have to first become aware of our spiritual origin, for every person is a child of the All-Highest, and should again become a pure being, a conscious son or daughter of the primordial, eternal life.

The right prayer leads us home to our origin, home into the kingdom of eternal light, where happiness, peace, harmony and bliss await us. Prayer is the bridge to the reality of the Spirit, to the life that sets us free.

Therefore, prayer has immeasurable power, since it connects us with the source of the strength of life, with the omnipotence of infinity, with God, our Father.

God is love. In prayer, the eternal current of power of the divine love, which is able to carry us upward to the loving consciousness of a spiritual life, to the heart of our primordial, eternal Father, takes hold of us more strongly.

However, the right way to pray has to be learned.

It is not lip-prayers that lead us to the promised land of inner life.

Words spoken without feeling do not open the floodgates of the inner being that cause the stream of eternal love to flow. It is not the wording, the length or other external aspects of prayer that matter. It is not in the word, in the letter, or in the sound alone that the power lies.

The right prayer takes shape from within. It flows from the soul and the heart. In the right prayer, the child addresses its Father in its inner being, that is, the child speaks to its inner God, until the floodgates open up through which the soul and heart then pray.

But how do I attain the right prayer, the divine consciousness, which constantly knocks at a person's heart and wants to reveal to him the inner fullness, the true origin? How do I attain the eternal reality, the life that makes me free?

The one who seeks will find. However, we cannot find the divine reality, the true peace and longed-for voice, outside of our consciousness, in this world.

In order to find this longed-for peace, the secureness and steadfastness, we must first find the way to ourselves. We should believe, that is, accept as truth and strengthen ourselves in the fact that we are not beings of this world, but beings who are on a journey heavenward, to the Kingdom of Peace.

Jesus of Nazareth said: "The Kingdom of God is within, in you." Therefore, we have to go into our inner being to find the peace and the love, for only the kingdom of the inner being, our eternal homeland, our original homeland, can again give us this peace and this stillness. To find the way to ourselves means: Recognize yourself!

Simple and plain as this sentence may seem, it becomes demanding for the one who sets out to actualize it. For nearly every one of us sees his surroundings and his fellow people through the eyes of his own ego. He looks, examines, evaluates and judges according to his very own criteria. There are many things and even many people we dislike, and we think and speak about them accordingly.

To find the way to ourselves means to no longer think negatively about our neighbor. Neither should we talk about them, how they are dressed, about their shortcomings, about the extent of their possessions, about what they do or say. We should look at ourselves and recognize our own faults and weaknesses, for what we find fault with in our neighbor is still in ourselves.

This fact, that there is in ourselves a correspondence to what we dislike in the other person, is a fundamental truth on the path of self-recognition. It is not easy for us to initially accept this fact.

Nevertheless, it is so, and soon it will be confirmed everywhere we go:

What we emit from our inner being is what we then discover outside of ourselves. Thus, each one has their world, totally according to their own way. And from what flows back to them, they can easily and surely recognize what they had sent out before.

If we would emit only love and were thus imbued with divine love, then only love would be expressed. However, if we preoccupy ourselves with our neighbor, with what we dislike about them, with what they think and do, or with the way they are dressed, we can conclude that similar things are in us. For if we were imbued with the love for God, we would emit only selflessness and love. But if envy, hatred and egocentricity are in us, we will emit what is still in us.

We mostly project these onto our neighbor, thinking that it is our neighbor, our colleague, our fellow person, who is tainted by this or that evil.

But in reality, we are what we want to attribute to our neighbor. For this reason, we should look at ourselves and recognize our own faults and weaknesses, so that we can get closer to our eternal being that is our true life.

I may repeat. The law of correspondence says: As long as we dislike something about our neighbor, it still shapes our nature; it is still present in ourselves.

Only through a disciplined life, by consistently attuning ourselves to the divine commandments and thus, to God, the Spirit of our inner being, will our soul, as well as each cell of our body attain peace and harmony, the stabilization in the awareness of God.

When we are increasingly able to find our way inward to the Kingdom of Peace, to our original homeland, by way of right prayer and meditation, we will be permeated and guided by the eternal power in us, fed and imbued by the life source of divine peace.

If we then place our trust more and more in the origin of our being, in God, we will become free of our human limitation, which was brought about by our intellectual thinking, feeling and wanting. We then become peaceful, harmonious and happy from within.

In order to find the origin of the wellspring, it is necessary to fight with ourselves. We must discard whatever hinders us from finding our way to where there is peace and harmony, where happiness and security permeate our whole being.

If we want to find peace, we should not plunge into the restlessness and bustle of this world. As often as possible, we should withdraw from all the sounds and noises of this world.

If it is possible for us to arrange a quiet room where we just pray and meditate, where we can have a dialogue with the divine, then this room will become a temple of divine harmony. A walk in a quiet forest of evergreen trees can also give us the blissful stillness to penetrate even deeper into the realm of eternal peace.

Nature gives so much strength and love to the conscious wayfarer; for nature serves the person who longs for God, for His stillness and His peace, giving the person powers upon powers. When we perceive nature with our external senses alone, then it reveals to us only its outer appearance: The grass, the flowers and the larger plants appear to be silent. Only the singing of the birds tells us that there is life in the trees.

But in reality, every blade of grass, every leaf, every needle of a fir tree sings the song of inner power. When we sit down on a bench or on a rock, away from the worldly bustle, and let the stillness of the woods, the stillness of our surroundings, have an effect on us, then we communicate with the harmonious and harmonizing forces of nature.

A person who practices this exercise frequently will come to realize that the right prayer is the right silence. When all negative thoughts have come to rest and our inner being rises toward the source of life, then right prayer takes place. Then praying is no longer thinking, but feeling the All-power in us, around us, and in all Being.

To find tranquility in God means to meet Him silently in us and in all Being.

God is the stillness.

It is said about Jesus that He withdrew into the stillness of nature to communicate with His Father. He recommended the same to His friends and to us all. He advised them and us to seek out a small quiet chamber, in order to hold a dialogue there with the Almighty. A true dialogue with God is deep, conscious, silent, selfless prayer.

So let us follow His instructions and withdraw for prayer into an undisturbed room or corner where the noises of the world, the harsh, coarse vibration of a noisy earthly life is silent.

But we should not be deceived by monastic practices, as a result of which many people think we must flee to a monastery or convent or to a cell, in order to find the inner stillness. This would merely be a flight from ourselves. It is not the flight from ourselves that leads us to God, but the return to ourselves, to the cell of our heart.

How do we find our way into this outer and inner stillness? We have to first learn the right silence, to attain a calm, harmonious body rhythm. Silence does not mean to merely close our mouth and not express our thoughts, while, however, retaining and moving them in us. Such a silence would be an external silence and would not bring us into the stillness.

The right silence means to let go of our thoughts about external things and people, about possessions, about money transactions, about meetings with our boss and with unpleasant colleagues. The right silence means to empty ourselves of everything trifling, of everything that preoccupies us again and again, which ultimately is our base self, our base nature.

When we learn to monitor our thinking and speaking and to distinguish the unessential from the essential, we will also succeed in coming into the right stillness, into the emptiness of thought that we need, so that the Spirit can fill us with His powers, with His love and wisdom.

How do we attain the right prayer, the perpetual thought of God, the stillness into which God, the stillness itself, speaks?

Again and again, we collect our thoughts and surrender them to God in order to become still. In this process of collecting our thoughts and surrendering the human being in us, we practice the right concentration.

To find our way to the true, deep prayer, there is no need for the usual practices and ceremonies of prayer. We need not fold our hands or put them together or even kneel down. For praying, we need not go to external places especially provided for this, like, for instance, churches. We also need not learn prayers by heart, nor recite them after someone or read them.

We have to become the prayer; it should pray within us. Words merely rambled on do not reach God. What constitutes prayer is not the words of our human language or the beautifully formed, well-considered sentences; but right prayer is the feelings, the vibrations of our soul and of our heart. Simple or even awkward words often express more than an intellectual prayer of contrived sentences. God hears only the longing of our heart, the deep resonance of our soul.

We need not keep to specific times for prayer, because God is always present everywhere. He is ready at every moment to accept the language of the soul and heart of His children.

He, the Almighty, perceives the impulses of our heart, and according to our devotion to Him, He blesses and strengthens us.

Right prayer is the constant closeness to God in feelings and thoughts. This is the prayer of depth, which is not spoken, but only felt, which means: We feel God in us, around us and in all Being.

If we want to learn to pray in the right way, much practice is necessary at first to become still. For this reason, when we first learn to pray, we should go to a quiet place where we are undisturbed, at best in the morning, before breakfast. With simple physical stretching exercises, which can be accompanied and supported by harmonious music, we attune our outer being, our body, as well as our inner being, our soul. Then we try to concentrate in this quiet, undisturbed place.

The following position helps us to achieve the best physical relaxation and inner concentration:

We sit on a straight-backed chair. Our torso rests upright on the coccyx. Both feet are on the floor. Our eyes are closed. We fold our hands in one another.

The left hand rests under the back of the right hand, and both palms are turned toward our body. In this way, we obtain a spiritual envelopment, in which the spiritual circulation is enclosed: Fingertips and palms do not radiate outward into our surroundings, but the energy flows back to the consciousness center located in the pelvic area. We remain still for some time in this position and surrender our ever-recurring thoughts to the eternal Spirit.

To free ourselves from this flood of thoughts, which seems to overwhelm us again and again, we can also use a so-called consciousness aid which has a high vibration and helps us become quieter, so that we can find our way deeper into our inner being. We say, for example, "Christ in me! Christ, become my life." Or "Harmony and peace draw into me. I am harmonious and peaceful."

In the beginning, we consciously assume the described position until it becomes a natural, harmonious prayer position for us.

During prayer we try to go from without to within, thus opening the floodgates to true inner prayer.

We now let our prayers of thankfulness and request flow inward to our spiritual consciousness. We continue to think the prayer into ourselves.

This prayer is still partly directed by our mind and flows, as mentioned, from without, from our person, from our brain cells, into our inner consciousness. Our prayer thoughts thereby touch our consciousness and our subconscious. They take along much to the divine, into the kingdom of the inner being, where we present our concerns. The eternal power that is active in the innermost part of our soul then transforms many things that we, consciously or unconsciously, place on the altar of divine love.

When first practicing the right prayer, we need support, and as help, an idea as to where to direct and send our prayers.

Thus, we imagine the altar of God in our chest, near the fourth consciousness center. On this inner altar of love and mercy, we place our prayers of thankfulness and petition, the streams of our consciousness and subconscious.

Furthermore, we can imagine that from the region of consciousness of Order, which is located in the pelvic area, the holy flame of God, the flame of salvation of life, flares up, touches our prayer thoughts, transforms them into holy and positive energies and directs them to where they can find entry and be effective.

The prayers that we still speak from our mind, and that we send inward, circle largely around our own interests. Only when we go more deeply into prayer, do we become aware that the entire fullness of infinity is in us and wants to become effective in us. When we then realize that we ourselves possess everything that we can open up through the right prayer and through a God-pleasing life, we will no longer ask, but will only give thanks.

Jesus said, "Ask and it will be given to you." In these words, we recognize that He was speaking to people on the level of Order who may well have had the fullness of life within them, but had not yet tapped into it.

Praying inward to the Spirit of God, to the spirit of the inner being, brings about the unification with the Spirit of God over the course of our lives, because to pray in the right way is the same as to live in the right way. What we do, we do in awareness of God, that is the nearness of God, that is the stream that guides and vivifies us.

Once we have found our way in this prayer to within, to God, to our inner consciousness—because the Spirit of God dwells in us—then, in the course of our spiritual exercises, it is also possible for us to thank, praise and glorify God from within.

Then our prayers also become more selfless, and the spiritual consciousness shows us that what we are asking for is actually already within us and has already been accomplished in us. God is in all things. He knows our desires even before we have brought them to Him. Nevertheless, we may request, so that we open up our inner being, the fullness that wants to become effective through us.

To pray within to God, to the holy consciousness, is a meditation of stillness, as it were. When we pray, we should do it slowly and consciously. A constrained prayer to achieve something or in the expectation of a particular result is a fruitless prayer.

We should allow the prayer thoughts to resonate in us slowly and harmoniously and get into the habit of taking a short pause after each sentence. Through this, we grow quieter and it helps us to find the way deeper into our spiritual consciousness, the inner God.

When we pray quietly and let our prayer feelings and thoughts build up in us, placing them on the altar of God, as it were, then no specific breathing technique is needed. Through a brief pause after each thought or spoken sentence, through a totally relaxed and calm breathing and a conscious opening for the Spirit, we experience inner peace. We thereby experience a unique kind of deep meditation, because the divine source in us responds as soon as we address it from the depths of our heart and filled with selfless love.

We should never forget that we are the temple of God and that the Spirit of our Father dwells in us. If we cleanse this temple, in that our thoughts are noble and our speaking and acting are like our thoughts, then we will find our way to the Spirit, to the Spirit of our Father—which not only dwells in the temple but also irradiates it.

Those who find the way to love by giving love will receive love in manifold ways. God, the eternal love, does not take. God is always the giving One. He, our Father, gives in abundance, for He is the fullness itself and also the fullness in us.

The Heart Prayer

The heart prayer is an intermediate step. Heart prayers flow from the soul garments, which show the longings and desires of the person. The heart prayer is therefore a prayer from the soul garments, prompted by the soul particles, which bear human aspects that still show the person's burdens. From there, the still existing longings and desires that rest in those deeper layers of the soul flow out.

Therefore, the heart prayer is still a wish-prayer, which, however, is deeper and is not shaped by the mind alone. A person praying from the heart is still before the gate to eternal bliss.

Heart prayers are like knocking at the gateway to the inner Kingdom of Peace and Love. The small steps, the steadfast striving, the repeatedly renewed devotion to the eternal power bring spiritual success here, too. The gate will be opened one day to the one who consistently practices the right prayer and the right way of living; he will penetrate deeper to the core of being in his soul, to the eternal consciousness of God.

In love and adoration, we should offer consciousness aids and prayers, indeed, our whole life, to Christ, who is our inner altar, our light, our life. He is the One who leads us to the Father. Thus, it is possible for everyone to journey toward their inner life, to the source of their being.

Through devotion and right prayer, in our inner being we distance ourselves from the world for some time. Once we have secured the necessary and conscious distance from the world through inwardness and right prayer, we can turn again to the world in a new way.

However, we attain this solely with practice, discipline and concentration and through our love for God and our neighbor, by turning within consciously to the holy consciousness of God. In this way, we prepare our person and soul, because the right, deep and selfless prayer and a fulfilled, lawful life lead to unity with all Being.

In this way, the wayfarer to the kingdom of life, to the inner homeland, is like a pilgrim who draws closer station by station to his inner God, to his inner homeland, thus attaining harmony and peace. The closer we come to the origin of the wellspring, the more we think and act from within, just as it corresponds to the eternal laws. Through this, we become conscious beings of the Almighty, sons and daughters of God, who know about the inner life and who then are no longer of this world, although they are still in the midst of the world.

Everyone is given the opportunity of a spiritual life in the midst of the world. Those who attain it are transformed from the ground up and gain a fulfilled existence through right prayer and a lawful life. Those who have tirelessly practiced heartfelt prayer will attain a harmonious body rhythm; their movements and gestures, their speech and actions will be more balanced and harmonious.

However, the goal of prayer should not remain the heart prayer, the constant knocking at the gate of the kingdom of the inner being. Over the course of time, our prayer should become the soul prayer, because the gate to salvation should open so that we may approach the origin of our life.

When the heart prayer has been largely perfected, the gate to the inner God opens slowly, and from the soul flow the first impulses of life, which then intermingle with the prayer of the heart.

This means that someone who has learned to immerse himself, by practicing the exercises of stillness and silence, already experiences, to some extent, streams from the soul, which mingle with the thoughts of the heart and form a prayer.

Once we have become people who think and pray from the heart, then the living power of our inner being rises up from this, welling up like living water, free of emotions, without compulsion. Then prayer brings joy, then it brings the longing to be connected with God at every moment, the longing for the nearness of God.

Every not yet fully purified soul, every person burdened with his ego is an individual who thinks and lives according to his mentality and attributes. This is why each person should pray in his own personal way, according to his present state of consciousness. Therefore, we should not imitate something that is not yet established in us; we should pray according to our own developed consciousness.

The right prayer is also a path of recognition; we recognize ourselves in our own prayer. As long as our prayer still contains desires and longings, we are still more or less strongly rooted in our ego.

We can recognize and free ourselves through the right prayer, provided that we surrender to the All-power what we have recognized and that we keep the laws. Then, as time passes, our prayer becomes selfless and a true melody of the inner being, which wells up from our stabilized consciousness and constantly attunes us anew, encouraging us to reach higher.

We should not adhere to prayer formulas; this just has a destructive effect on our own consciousness.

We should pray according to our attributes, our momentary feelings and thoughts. Even prayers that are usually said on certain occasions merely impose constraints on us.

True seekers, those who pray from the heart, who also recognize themselves in prayer, will find their way to the inner source only when they pray freely, when they let their consciousness pray. A free prayer rises up from a loving heart and from a soul that opens itself for God, our Lord.

In order to let the prayer flow from our heart, we must become still and turn off our thoughts completely. So that our thoughts move away from us, we listen to our breathing before praying and observe our body rhythm, which becomes more and more harmonious. Our breathing becomes calmer and our movements more harmonious, because the tormenting thoughts leave us. We achieve a quiet body rhythm, because our breathing grows deeper.

Once we have been able to let go of our thoughts, once they have left us, we no longer watch our breathing or our body rhythm. We are now ready to pray from our heart, to let forces of love flow.

If it is not yet possible for us to carry out the heart prayer, then we pray into our inner being until forces stir within us that then pray through us. We pray into ourselves. We place our concerns—including what burdens and oppresses us—on the altar of God.

Once we are stable within ourselves, it will then pray in us. Selfless prayers will then rise without effort. It is a process of letting the inner powers come, which develop into prayer sensations and prayer thoughts. It prays through us.

This heart prayer, combined with the streams of the soul, characterizes the state in which our prayer clearly becomes one with our thinking, feeling and wanting. Therefore, it is no longer the prayer from the intellect, but the prayer from the uppermost layers of our spiritual consciousness.

This transition from praying with effort, with its reflections and formulations, to praying independently is a deep, unmistakable experience in the innermost part of our being.

We have to find our way to the depths of our being, where the awakened soul is in constant adoration of God. Then the prayer speaks in us, no matter where we are—in our quiet room or in the noisy world. It prays in and through us.

Then we have attained the nearness to God. The soul has awakened in God, and the person is aligned with God. This means that soul and person are near the eternal consciousness, God.

The one who has practiced the heart prayer with utmost discipline, concentration and exercises to attain stillness senses the love of the All-ruling Spirit. Through the power of this love, he finds his way to this unceasing prayer, which rises at any time, any place, out of his inner be-ing, giving thanks, honor and praise to God.

God is everywhere, for the Spirit of God is in us and in everything that surrounds us. Nothing exists with-out the eternal power, God. For this reason, we can constantly speak with

God, be it during housework, at our job, on the road, on a bus or train or on a walk. In every activity, God, the All-power, is active in and around us.

If we act nobly and kindly, if our feelings and thoughts are pure, then this is likewise a prayer, for we fulfill the law of love. In this way, too, it prays through us.

Before we go to sleep or right after awakening it will pray in and through us, because our thought is like the thought of God. This is how we find our way to true prayer, for each one of us should become the prayer.

Those who do these spiritual exercises of praying to within so that the gate to life may open, consciously and out of love for God, are grasped by prayer, so that the whole person prays, no matter where they are. Only once we have become the prayer do we actualize the laws in the right way, because fulfilling the holy laws is the same as the right prayer. There are enough people who pray regularly, who pray with their lips, but there are few who live in the nearness of God and have become the prayer.

On our pilgrimage to our inner God—which goes by way of becoming still, by way of the heart prayer, meditative contemplation and a conscious, lawful life—we become capable of sensing and feeling ethereally. This means that we become more sensitive, more permeable to the eternally holy power. Then it is possible for us to feel within ourselves the substance of our true life, the holy power that is active in all things.

We are beings of light and have to ascend the ladder to heaven—via which we once descended into the valley of tears and bitterness—in order to reunite with God, our Father. This ascent up the ladder of cosmic life is like a journey into the eternal Kingdom of God, which is within us.

We can climb the rungs to the cosmic consciousness only when we love God above all else. The Eternal's love then gives us the strength to live lawfully, to think and act in a disciplined manner and to work with concentration so that we may become still through inner silence. Then, through the heart prayer and the soul prayer, we arrive at the ether prayer, which completely unites us with the Eternal.

By journeying to the kingdom of the inner being, we become selfless. Those who have become selfless no longer think of themselves; they give. Then our prayer, too, is similar. We no longer pray for our own concerns.

We know that we have everything, that the fullness offers itself to us every day. We pray for our neighbor, for the world, so that it may awaken and also find its way to the inner fullness, to God, who takes care of us, who is there for us. Our innate, cosmic, divine love then awakens more and more and gives us freedom and the deep peace that the world does not know, although many people seek it.

When we speak of the heart prayer, we do not mean the central anatomical organ, the physical heart of the human being, but the heart we mean is the living life, the realization that God exists—to whom we offer our thoughts and feelings, so that it is not merely our intellect, our human consciousness that prays, or even our subconscious, but rather the streams of the awakened soul that are praying.

However, we do not want to stay with the heart prayer; this would be a standstill in our spiritual development. We want to reach the highest goal, the ether prayer, the constant nearness to God, indeed, the fulfillment of what is lawful.

The heart prayer is the same as knocking at the inner gate that leads to the throne room of God, to His immediate heart.

The heart prayer is merely a pre-liminary step toward the soul prayer and the ether prayer. We want to strive to reach that highest goal, the unification with the consciousness of God.

Those who live in the high, constant adoration and praise of God, who thank and glorify Him for all things and fate live near to God. All things in life are evident to them, because they have found their way to the inner truth.

Once we have opened the inner floodgates to the consciousness of God, once the gate to deeper bliss has opened, we will then advance toward the sensation of the soul, which conveys a high form of prayer to us.

Once we have advanced into deeper spheres of inner stillness, by praying the heart prayer into us and letting it rise back toward us, we then experience the prayer of the soul and of the heart, whereby soul and heart blend into one another. We could also describe this as follows: Filled with spiritual power, the consciousness and the subconscious are united with the soul. Soul and body worship the Godhead.

It should be our goal that our entire thinking, speaking and acting

take place from the spiritual consciousness, that it thinks, speaks and
acts through us. We will find our way
to this high goal when we attune ourselves through ever deeper prayer,
and by acting accordingly in our ev-
eryday life.

The further form of inner prayer
is that we place everything we think
and do on our opened consciousness,
on the spiritual potential we have developed, which has taken shape in us
through a spiritual life.

Then it becomes possible for us to
live more and more in the realm of
our inner being and also to receive

consciously from there for our material existence. Then we no longer live externally, tormented and hounded by fear and opinions, shaped and dependent on our way of thinking and acting and on our intellect. Instead, we live consciously from God, because God can work through us, because He, the Almighty, directs our body, matter and all our thinking and striving, thus guiding us. It, the life, guides us.

If we attain the nearness to God in our thinking, feeling, speaking and wanting, we will bear His holy name continuously and consciously in us. Then our prayers will increase in love, purity, selflessness, peace and obedience, and we will soar, as it were, to further heights in order to pray in an even more fulfilled way.

The Soul Prayer

Complicated forms of prayer are tiring and distract us, because they come from human realms, from our world of thoughts and senses, shaped by our desires and longings. What has been acquired over years comes from without. This also applies to prayer. What lies in the depths of our soul is spiritually innate in us and comes from the pure regions of our soul. These innermost streams free person and soul.

The path to the inner life demands a constant, critical observation of our feeling, thinking and acting. We have to avoid negative feelings and thoughts. They cloud our consciousness and bind us to external forms of prayer and to prayers that bear our own longings and desires. Then it no longer prays in us, but it is our intellect that prays. What the intellect produces does not bring about the nearness to God.

So that it may pray, think, speak and act through us, we have to watch our thoughts, to train our will, and to place our whole way of living under the protection of the seal of divine Love.

The autonomous prayer of the soul flows only after a continuous, earnest and conscious struggle for the inner love and freedom.

Everything is grace; everything come from the Giver of life. Thus, the soul prayer, too, is a gift of God, which He grants to those who love Him more than this world. The soul prayer is the prayer of the selfless person. It cannot be achieved through certain techniques. It is given to those who strive for the inner God in all earnestness and always conscientiously monitor themselves, in order to become selfless.

The soul prayer is a prayer of the soul, of the heart and body. If we have attained a deep tranquility and stillness, if we can remain silent in thoughts and words when our neighbor talks and boasts of his abilities and qualities, and if we can remain quiet in the midst of our daily life, in the bustle of this world, then we have made great progress. We have taken a few steps toward self-mastery on the path to spirituality.

We will then be filled from within, as it were, with strength and life and will continue to be oriented toward the highest goal. Through our increased strength, we will also be able to recognize the deeper-lying shadows of the human ego and to conquer them. We will then be fulfilled through the nearness to God and will pray from the soul, as it reveals itself there, in the deeper regions of stillness.

Once the soul has established a deep communion with God, our Father in Christ, and is filled with His presence, then we will rest more and more in God, our Lord. Then there is no longer any need for consciousness aids, nor for watching our breathing and even less for certain forms of prayer. By way of deep stillness, we increasingly receive the streams from the consciousness of the soul.

When heart and soul are filled with the omnipotence of God, they allow no more sinful thoughts or unlawful ideas.

If a person lives in the deep thought of God, then a transformation has taken place in his life. He has gained distance from the world by becoming aware of and loosening the ties that spiritually interwove him with the world, thus holding him captive. Strengthened and stabilized in his inner being, he can now approach the world again in a different way. Through such a way of life, through right prayer and a lawful life, we have found the path that shows us, often after a long search, the possibility of a spiritual life in the midst of the world.

For the one who rests in God, there are no longer differences among in his fellow people, but only children, sons and daughters of the eternal Father, who are on the way to the inner homeland. The one who lives in this high sensation of the All-unity is linked not only with people and beings, but with infinity. He beholds the life in all things and worships it. Thus, he is also close to the divine in nature. He feels himself to be the essence in every tree, in every bush, in every flower. He feels himself to be the essence in the stars, indeed, in all Being, and he senses that the essence of all Being is in him.

This communication of forces, which is like a true "communion," is the deep prayer, the prayer of the soul, which introduces the ether prayer.

The person who lives in this consciousness henceforth sees only the workings of the eternal laws in all things. He radiates love and kindles love in his fellow human beings. He stands above the vicissitudes of human life and is without fear. Nothing of low vibration penetrates him. Step by step, this high goal is reached. His life and work become a blessing from God, and his prayers bear fruit.

The soul prayer flows of its own accord. It flows from the inner being without effort. It is a selfless prayer, a prayer of tranquility, a prayer of union with the forces of love in the soul and in all Being. This prayer brings stability and support, for it is not spoken by us, the intellect, but flows from our opened spiritual consciousness, from our present, re-gained spiritual power potential.

When the soul has absorbed the conscious prayer thoughts of Christ and is filled by His presence, the gate to the eternal life can also open further, so that ever more rays of divine love may penetrate it and fill the person's body with light.

In the heart prayer and the soul prayer, we experience clearly and distinctly the statement: "I stand at the door and knock. If a person hears My voice and the door opens through prayer and love, I will enter, and I will be with him, and he will be with Me, and his supper will be My supper."

By praying to within, by asking for strength, we come to the heart prayer, through which we find our way to the inner prayer, by letting it pray, as it were. In this sequence—praying within and letting it pray—we reach the soul prayer. In this way, we reach the gateway, which the Lord Himself opens to us.

The soul prayer is no longer the heart prayer, in which the person and part-streams of the soul ask for their concerns and repeatedly present their needs. The soul prayer is much more. It embraces the entirety, since the soul praises and glorifies God in Christ through the person.

The pure soul prayer without the secondary influences of human wanting is an adoration and a veneration of the All-Highest, who knows about all things and is all things.

The soul prayer is deeply rooted. It feels, thinks, speaks and acts through me; it prays through me.

The soul prayer is praying from the opened consciousness, from the soul's spiritual potential of forces, which the person has actualized through a life in and with God. The first streams of the mentality of the inner being, of the spirit being, can be in the soul prayer.

In the final analysis, everything is filled and borne by the holy consciousness, God, the core of being of life. This is also true of the soul prayer. The Spirit of God radiates into the soul, and the luminous being, the largely purified soul, shows its spiritual origin, its mentality, in prayer. The purer the soul is, the more selfless and sublime is the soul prayer.

The difference between the heart prayer and the soul prayer becomes very clear. The one who has found his way to the true soul prayer is selfless. He knows that all things are in him: What he asks for, he already has; what he desires, he already possesses.

Through these recognitions and by fulfilling the Will of God, the person, the small, base ego, withdraws. The personal concerns withdraw and the awakened, light-filled soul praises and thanks God. It speaks to Him in pure and noble feelings, thoughts and words.

When the noble, pure and beautiful emanate from us, we increasingly find our way to the deep, genuine, selfless soul prayer. The awakened soul continuously thanks God, God, the Giver, who at the same time is the gift, since He unites all good things in Himself. If we are ill, He is our healer. If we are hungry, He feeds us. If we are cold, He warms us. If we are accused, He defends us. If we are insulted, He comforts us. If we are persecuted, He is our rescue. If we have fallen, He picks us up. If we doubt,

He strengthens us. If we become inconsistent and weak, He gives us courage.

From this, we recognize that we are the limbs on the spiritual body of Christ and, at the same time, cells on His spiritual body. If His name is close to us, if we are constantly linked with Him in thought, that is, if our feelings and thoughts are pure, we will be imbued by His holy power. The one who recognizes His ruling hand in everything communicates with the holy forces, which are active in the minerals, in the plants, in the animals and especially in human beings.

God lives through the one who lives in Him, and He lets become manifest everything that the soul hides from the one who strives for only outer things and lives externally.

Once a person has found this power of prayer, he is filled with the natures and attributes of God, and gradually becomes the prayer. The one who has become the prayer is selfless and no longer marked by his ego. The one who rests in God, his Lord, has surrendered his ego to the *I Am*, the great Spirit who knows all things.

In God, human things are unimportant and trivial. What is important is the law, which is the fullness and brings out the fullness in us. The one who lives in the fullness of God is fearless, for he lives in the truth. God is the truth.

In the course of his becoming, the one who strives for God will let go of everything unessential that distances him from the divine stream of salvation, that distracts him and wants to pull him down into the world of illusions.

The one who wants to prepare his whole soul for the deep prayer, the soul prayer, should send awakening impulses over and over again into his innermost being, into the soul, for example:

Father,
You are my innermost conscious-
ness! Holy and mighty is Your
eternal love.

Through the consciousness of
Your Son, Jesus Christ, I experience
Your holy natures and attributes
in myself.
Your "Let there be" streams through
my soul, so that I may become
what I am from the very beginning.
Let me become the prayer;
let me be wholly Yours.

My soul, lift your voice in praise of
the One who created you!

May my soul praise, glorify and
thank the Lord, the Almighty, who
is all things and in everything.

Hallowed is His name.
I sanctify His name, so that
I may be divine again through
His name, God.

Resting in our innermost being, turned away from external phenomena, we listen for the impulses of the soul. Patient and ready, without wanting anything and totally prepared for God, we await the prayer of our soul.

Our linking in thought with the eternal Spirit in us brings us closer to the Omnipresence. If we call His name fervently, God will answer us.

If the soul has taken in the thought on the Christ of God and is filled with His presence, then every thought will be a thought in Christ, since every thought is a thought of salvation, noble and pure. Then it is not necessary to constantly repeat the name of Christ, for we live in Him and He lives through us.

Repeating the name of God and of the Christ of God is indicated only when we are drawn outward again by the events of this side of life. When we experience hardship, distress or fear, we should pronounce the names "God-Father" or "Christ" with calmness and hope, trusting in the All-power that we will receive what we ask for. This invocation is successful only if we ask selflessly, if we do not want to force anything, but rather place it before the Almighty so that He may order it according to His will.

If we are tempted by the world, by external forms, by images and impressions, then we should persistently, but calmly call on the name of God and of the Christ of God and turn away from external influences in our thoughts.

We let the melody "Father" or "Christ" build up in our heart and in our soul, until all thoughts of doubt, fear, anxiety and all negative feelings flow out of our inner being and we may once again feel the inflow of the All-power and, anew and strengthened, receive His light.

It is a blessing to be united with the Eternal! If our thoughts are close to God, then we feel the rescuing hand of the Almighty at every moment.

If we do not just keep His name on our lips, but let it flow through our whole being, then the might and power of the Godhead becomes visible through us, because our life is marked by spiritual success. We will fulfill in the world what is for the benefit of our neighbor, of his soul. This inner, divine power of love then also dominates our entire physical body, strengthening and fortifying us. It keeps away from us what is typical of the world: illness, hardship and worry. The fulfillment of the holy laws purifies our soul, our heart and our body and sanctifies our being.

Equipped with these forces, we will pray more and more consciously, and, in the end, find our way to the ether prayer, in which we are absolutely filled with the omnipresent power of God.

Through this development in prayer and by fulfilling the spiritual life, we find our way more and more to the eternal consciousness, to the core of being of God in our soul.

Once we let go of our person, our base ego, and lead a conscious inner life, we will find unification with God and will consciously be in God, and we will be conscious of God in us— and we will become the law, the being that God created, the divine being.

The Ether Prayer

The ether prayer is the recognition and, at the same time, the absolute fulfillment of the holy laws of God.

With our daily effort to be pleasing to God, we penetrate ever deeper into the kingdom of our inner being.

By going steadily within, to our inner God, to the kingdom of the inner being, about which Jesus said, "My kingdom is not of this world," we come to ever greater regions of sublime stillness and deep peace.

If we no longer struggle with ourselves, our soul has become very still and we rest in God, our Lord. We can then say consciously and with absolute certainty, "It is not I who live, but Christ lives and works through me."

In this vivifying state of true, deep stillness and divine joy, we climb the last slope toward the Absoluteness, toward the perfect truth. In this state of constant inwardness, we can be in the midst of the greatest turmoil, in a world full of noise—and yet remain quiet, turned into our inner being, since our soul has become still. It rests in God, its Lord, who created it. Then it is no longer we who live, but it lives through us.

The person who experiences this state of unity with God is united from within with the absolute consciousness, God. He is guided by God, the All-power, without the interposition of the soul garments and of the conscious mind and the subconscious.

Then it is not we who think and act, but it feels, thinks, speaks and acts through us. Thus, we become the true prayer; we become the prayer itself, which lasts forever, for the eternally holy law of Love created us. We came from Him and must find our way back to Him, and become the absolute law.

We attain the tranquility and inner stability, indeed, the stillness of our soul, only by purposely going within to our eternal consciousness, which waits for us, as it were, which calls us, and which we should become again. By going within to our holy consciousness, to God, our eternal Father, by way of the heart prayer and the soul prayer and the fulfillment of the inner life, we experience the presence of the Father and of the Son in us and in every person.

Those who live in Christ find themselves in the true temple, for the human being is the temple of the Holy Spirit.

Through this life out of the inner being, we experience more and more the great unity in God. We learn that all life comes from His holy consciousness, that He is the life in all things. People who experience this depth, the stillness of their soul, know that they are linked in love with those who already live in the beyond and are going toward further liberation and development. In this way, we grow more and more into the unity of God and ultimately become the unity.

During this steady blossoming in the holy law of God, we come to know and experience the presence of all life more each day, and from this, we recognize that everything is in us and we are in everything. Someone who experiences this and attains the fulfillment from the stream of life has found their way home.

Through this knowledge, the fulfillment and the awakening in the eternal law of unity, of divine love, we come to know and experience ever deeper peace and vivifying harmony, for we draw closer to the origin of the wellspring, to the Absolute.

In the divine peace and the divine harmony, which are also the stillness of our inner being, the envelopments of humanness fall from us more and more. Fear, vanity and blind egocentricity are far from us, for we have become the true and deep prayer.

This becoming brings us selflessness, because we are consciously born in God, just as Christ, the Redeemer-Spirit, is innate in us.

Feeling more than thinking, we then approach our fellow people, on the street, in the office, in the store, in the workshop or automobile.

We recognize Christ in all people, even in those whom we find disagreeable and unpleasant. When we see Christ even in our apparent enemies, when we see our brother and sister in them, then we show greatness and may say, "We are becoming one with the holy primordial principle; we are getting closer to the origin of the source."

The inner stillness tells us: Honor your heavenly Father in Christ and serve Him in each of your fellow people; for in all men and women, even in the wicked and criminal, dwells the Spirit of your Father in Christ, the healing and redeeming flame, implanted through the sacrifice on Golgotha.

Let us realize that we are all brothers and sisters and will one day meet again in the eternal homeland as pure children of the eternal Father! If we strive for this already now on Earth, then we will have nothing more to forgive in the realms beyond and nothing that needs to be forgiven. We are free in God, happy in the eternal homeland, which is our eternal destination.

Therefore, we should endeavor to address Christ in our neighbor, no matter how they feel about us, by silently acknowledging Christ in them. Then the human aspects will recede more and more and we will behold our brother and sister in Christ through our spiritual eyes.

If we go through the world with this spiritual attitude and say only good and noble things about our fellow people, if we see in everything the holy workings of God, the workings of His heavenly laws, and if we strive to fulfill them in ourselves, in our neighbor and also in the nature kingdoms, then we are walking in the law of the Almighty and thus fulfilling the ether prayer: "I am in God, and God is consciously in me, working through me."

The more we are ready to recognize the ruling hand of God in all things, to thank Him, to praise and glorify Him and bear His name in our heart and on our lips, the more radiant our soul becomes, the brighter our disposition. We then fulfill what the Almighty desires of us, His children: that we subdue the Earth in love. This is deep prayer; this is the ether prayer.

The one who lives in the ether prayer lives henceforth from within. His inner homeland is already wide open to him. From now on, his sensing, thinking, speaking, feeling and acting take place via his expanded and stabilized mental and spiritual consciousness.

What he thinks and says is no longer his intellect, his mind, but his innermost consciousness, the law of the soul. The active consciousness of our soul then acts on our physical consciousness and conveys the inner life to us. The conscious child of God, living in the "I am the son or the daughter of the Most High," then faithfully fulfills the impulses of their soul.

Those who live in the divine consciousness in this way will think and speak only good and essential things. Their speech is no longer directed by their mind. Although they speak with the words of this world, it is, nevertheless, a different language, a thoroughly spiritualized and refined language, which flows, so to speak, from their inner being. It is the language of the divine consciousness.

Those who want to cast off the shackles forged by error should walk this path of prayer and of the fulfillment of the holy laws. Only in this way, will the God-seeker find his way to the absolute truth; and after the temporal, his soul, which has become a pure spirit-body, will see God, its Father, face to face. The one who has the fervent faith in the inner power and strength of the eternally Holy One and consciously bears Him in his heart day and night needs no further spiritual exercises.

The true Christian, who lives from his opened inner consciousness, recognizes that in the end all paths merge in Christ and lead through Christ to the Father. If Christ has risen in us, we will be kind to all people.

The absolute ether prayer, the deep true prayer, is when we no longer know that we are praying because we are continuously fulfilling the holy laws. We then live constantly in the spirit of truth; we feel, think and speak from the inner truth. Our actions arise from the truth.

Then there will no longer be hollow and flat expressions, no empty forms, no lies, no sentimentality. Our feelings and impulses are then genuine, as genuine as every tear that is shed when the sweetness and glory of God completely permeate us. Then our tears become pearls that point the way to absolute omnipotence. They bring us strength and higher spirituality.

But without an inner struggle, we will not find the way to our inner life, to the deep stillness of God. We are called upon to struggle with our weaknesses and faults. However, with the inner power, with the power of Christ, we will conquer ourselves, thus becoming blessed people who want to bless all people, not with many words, not through fanaticism, but through a conscious life and by explaining the true inner "religion."

Once we constantly think of God in our soul, in our heart and on our lips, we have become a prayer and are before the absolute unification with the eternal Being, with God, our Father. Then, the soul, our purified body, will cry out through us: "Father, into your hands I commend my spirit. It is finished through Christ."

The Healing Prayer

Pray yourself healthy! The best help for your health, which is the life force, is positive, noble feelings and thoughts. The nobler and purer your inner attitude, the more forces of healing and of life you awaken.

Christ, the spark of life in you, is the power of healing and life of your soul and of your body. When you open the inner gateway to the Kingdom of God with the redeeming power of Christ, by affirming healing, even the healing forces, and by fulfilling the holy laws, then you will also receive. Pray yourself healthy!

Let every feeling, every thought and every word become a prayer! Then the gate to life will open, and you will be filled with strength, wisdom, love and health.

It is written, "Ask and it will be given to you." However, the request should not be the mere expression of an external affirmation, a call or a lip prayer. The request should come from the fulfillment of the holy laws, from the affirmation of the inner strength through a refined way of feeling, thinking and wanting.

The eternal life energy flows unceasingly from the source of the wellspring. If we accept it willingly by fulfilling the laws, we receive this healing and life-giving force via the core of being of our soul. We can increase the inflow of this healing and life-giving force many times over if we affirm these forces of life and fulfill them in our daily life, since they are the laws of life.

If we knock at the gate to eternal life by raising our hearts to God, the gate will open and it will be given to us.

An inner prayer to the Inner Physician and Healer requires strong faith and deep trust in the One who can do everything, who is everything. To become healthy means to become healthy through the power of the Inner Physician and Healer.

The Spirit of God knows no illness; and according to our origin, we are pure beings who bear within all the powers of salvation. As beings of light, we are not sick. We are sick because of our wrong thinking, feeling and wanting, because of our violations of the law. However, through Christ it is given to us to address the inner forces, to activate them and also to lead them to the sick or unhealthy organs concerned, because according to our origin we are children of God.

Since we are children of the eternal life, sons and daughters of God, it is given to us to direct the forces of healing and of life to every organ, to every muscle, to our whole organism through the right prayer and by addressing the organs. Each one of us can speak with their cells and organs, since the spiritual power is in every cell. The more intensely we affirm this inner power through a strong faith and total trust, through positive thoughts, refined feelings and the fulfillment of the holy laws, the more we will receive.

With a conscious inner prayer, with positive feelings and thoughts, a wake-up call is made to our cells and organs, to our entire organism. When we continuously affirm the inner forces, the forces of healing and of life, with our opened consciousness—that is, in full affirmation—then a change occurs in us. The Inner Physician and Healer, the Spirit of Christ, then becomes increasingly active.

The eternal power, Christ, is simply waiting until we are willing to open the inner gate with Him through the power of right prayer and the right will, in order to thus surrender to the inflow of the eternal divine potential.

We are cells on the body of Christ. Our body cells are ailing merely because we have weakened them through wrong thinking, feeling and wanting, thus granting certain illnesses entry. If we send positive, healthy, light-filled thoughts to our cells, organs, tissues and muscles, our hormones and glands, we will then receive from the eternal source of life according to our devotion.

Therefore, the best help for your health is positive, selfless thoughts; they are the building material for a healthy body. If we daily affirm the health of our body, no illness can enter us, when there is no correspondence in us, unless the illness is determined by karma.

If we fall ill, recovery is always granted to us, when it is good for our soul. If we open the inner gate to life with Christ, through an affirmative life willed by God, then we receive, for the Inner Physician and Healer dwells in us. He waits for our call, for our turning to Him, for the actualization and fulfillment of the laws, because then the gate opens and life flows into our body as a current, bringing us relief and healing.

God's love for His child is immutable. It is not He, the almighty

Love, who sends us suffering and hardship—they are based solely on the omnipotent and universal law of cause and effect, on the law of justice. In this life or in one of our previous lives, we created causes and became guilty of violating the law. We have to accept and bear whatever we cause, so that the way back to the light-filled eternal origin, to the eternal home-land, can be walked again.

A soul-debt that flows out in our lives according to iron laws bringing us illness, hardship, worries or blows of fate can, nevertheless, be healed or alleviated, depending on the severity of the karma. The extent to which it can be paid off depends solely on us, on how we surrender to the Inner Physician and Healer, the Spirit of Christ, whether in full trust and faith in Him, the Almighty, or doubting whether He is able to help and heal us. Every doubt is a step backward in our lives. It closes us off and cements over the gate that leads to the Inner Physician and Healer. Affirmative, conscious, single-minded thoughts on God lead to success.

The condition of our body is the expression of our soul, of our present or former sensing, thinking, feeling and wanting. What we think today is what we are in our inner being; it is our nature; it is the thoughts we have thought into this or in a former life. In this way, we created the correspondence in us, the burden of our soul.

No illness comes of itself, we are always guilty of it. The so-called chronic diseases are likewise visible manifestations of our former or current negative thoughts.

If we want to bring about a change, we should reflect on the Inner Physician and Healer and entrust ourselves to Him, by persistently and consciously thinking positively, thus mobilizing the inner forces.

Healing prayers are mostly prayers of request. They should flow from the depths of our consciousness; then they are powerful and can bring healing. However, when we pray and request, we should not beg.

A wailing request for this or that, for health and strength does not take place in the consciousness of true, sincere humility; it is not addressed to the great Giver, who would like to grant His child all the good that it needs. However, the omnipotent, omniscient Spirit of God knows best what is helpful and beneficial for us at present.

Thus, we do not ask a God who first has to be well-disposed and favorably inclined toward us to grant our request, but should ask our heavenly Father, whose Spirit we know dwells in us. We should fully trust Him, no matter whether He considers our soul alone, or both our soul and body. When we affirm His eternal power thankfully and gladly, it will also permeate us.

The spirit of love is the power of our life; it is the healing power for soul and body. This power alone lets us become happy, whole and perfect.

The healing prayer should not be limited to a prayer request, but should become a continuous affirmation of the divine energies in us.

We should not grant access to any thought of despondency, weakness, sorrow or lack of faith. They merely weaken our soul and our body. Our consciousness and subconscious, the surface of the inner sea, should become calm, so that the inner sun is able to heal us.

When we become accustomed to replacing thoughts of misery, fear, desperation, hopelessness, despondency and self-pity with positive, affirmative thoughts, then we will also have a positive harvest. For the sunny brightness of our life lets the inner sun shine more intensely into our body, to our cells, organs and muscles.

As long as we see ourselves as human beings and think as human beings, we have only the powers of human beings. But when we acknowledge ourselves as children of the Almighty, as divine beings, when we think in a positive and refined way, when we direct our thoughts and aspirations toward God, then we attain the powers of our primordial, eternal being. We may rely on God, our Father, for we are sons and daughters of God.

A healing prayer is the complete affirmation of health, which is our God-given right, since the divine being that we are in our innermost being is healthy.

Even when pain torments us, when our soul is clouded, we should, despite everything, think into ourselves forces of health, affirming, positive, constructive thoughts. That is the best medicine; it is the forces not yet scientifically explored that take effect in our inner being.

A healing prayer may read as follows:

In me is the Spirit of Christ,
the absolute eternal power.
Within me flow
the wellsprings of life.
I am healthy.
I am a child of this eternal power.
God's life is in me,
and my life is in God.

God's fullness is effective in me.
God is the fullness and the power.
God is my health.
His holy and healing power floods
through my soul and my body
and makes everything new.

My cells, organs, hormones
and glands, the muscles and tissues
are permeated by the spiritual
power and pervaded
by the holy life forces.

I affirm this eternal power in me
and open myself each day more for
the life in me through affirming,
constructive feelings and thoughts.
Weakness and illness
do not touch me,
for my eternal being is healthy.

I am healthy;
I am full of the zest for life
and strong.

I feel the increasing inflow
of the divine fullness.
The eternally bubbling wellspring
fulfills itself in me. I receive
from it increased strength,
health and fullness.
All thoughts of worry and fear
withdraw from me.
They become ever weaker
and dissolve in the
All-harmony of my Father.

From my inner being
rises the divine stillness.

I am permeated by the inner
stillness and All-harmony.

Vivified by this inner calm,
I turn increasingly toward
the inner healing power.
The healing and life forces
flow through me more each day.
The Redeemer-Spirit, Christ,
is effective in me, my
Inner Physician and Healer.

My hands and arms relax;
the muscles of my legs loosen.
My whole body, my throat, neck
and head, all the muscles relax.
My body becomes lighter
and lighter.

The fullness of divine salvation
flows into me.

Healing forces of love activate me.
My breathing is calm;
I am totally relaxed.

Inner tranquility and harmony
permeate my being.

Christ, You, my Inner Physician
and Healer, may Your will be
done in me.

After this healing prayer, we remain in the stillness. No feeling and no thought flows through us. We are and remain open to the healing forces of Christ.

So that no thoughts find their way into us, we may watch our breathing while absolutely relaxed, how it comes and goes again.

With every inhalation, the divine power flows into our inner being; with every exhalation, the heaviness and burden, our still remaining human weaknesses and afflictions are released.

It is done in us according to His will.

In us the Inner Physician and Healer accomplishes the work of His love and mercy.

After the healing prayer and being in the stillness, we should no longer let ourselves be dominated by our old habits. We should strive to affirm all the positive forces that we have set free in our inner being with further prayers that bring healing and through a positive life. When we avoid every negative thought, any thought of illness and affliction, we experience increased spiritual power. We experience the inner healing power, which gives us relief and healing.

Many of our fellow people think they have to visit a place of healing in order to be healed of their suffering—they often travel many miles to such places, taking on the hardships in order to possibly obtain relief or healing there.

But those who know that the place of inner strength is in themselves—from which they can receive what is good and beneficial for them—need only to go on their own inner pilgrimage, to the inner place of holy stillness and eternal peace in their inner being, where the wellspring of healing and of life flows.

Whether we are in a place of healing or elsewhere, the power is always the same. It is not outside our being, but in us. Wherever we are, wherever we go, the source of healing for all life, the strength to attain health, is in us. Within us is the spring of health, the Spirit.

When cases of spontaneous healing take place in such places of healing, it is only because the people make a pilgrimage there with the certainty of a strong faith, to attain healing there. If those seeking healing would make a pilgrimage to the inner place of grace, to the inner source of healing, with the same trust and vivified by this deep faith, they could also receive relief and healing from their inner being.

The power of life flows eternally in the same way, at any place and at any time. God, the source of life, is not tied to any place. The divine stream is omnipresent. God, the eternal Spirit, gives Himself to His children.

We have to recognize and acknowledge that the power for becoming healed is in us. It is granted to us only if we open ourselves for it. What hinders us from obtaining relief and healing is, above all, our lack of faith.

Jesus could hardly bring about a healing in Nazareth, His hometown, because the Nazarenes did not believe in Jesus, who had grown up there.

All things are possible to the one who believes and fulfills the divine laws. The harvest always corresponds to the sowing.

If sowing positive and trusting thoughts is slight, the result of relief and healing is also slight. Another hindrance is doubt. People who doubt do not look within themselves, but to the right and left. They look to this world for healing.

Many people waver between believing and disbelieving, because they have not been taught since childhood that they are the temple of the Holy Spirit and that the source of all Being, the source of healing, flows in them. Through this, they set up barriers against the divine inflow. They search externally for relief and healing and mostly cannot find what their soul needs.

How quickly we become discouraged when our prayer requests are not immediately heard as we would like or as we had experienced before!

Let us consider how long we have sinned against the holy laws, thus creating a gap between the divine power and our own thinking and feeling.

The Holy Spirit does not act immediately, for it is necessary that we ourselves overcome this gap so that the healing streams can flow.

And, not every day is like another, and we ourselves are not the same every day. In us, in our inner being, there are many kinds of changes that are partially hidden to us, and that can likewise erect a barrier against the inflow of the healing power in us.

The right prayer, a deep prayer, is indeed important in order to be heard. However, we should not want to achieve anything with it, for prayer is not a sport, but devotion.

Let us help to put order again in our inner being by continually bearing thoughts of God in our heart and on our lips, by doing everything with God, and praising His holy name, His holy law, which prevails in all things! Many a knot, which may have hardened during long years on Earth or even over many incarnations, can be undone only gently with divine Patience, Love and Mercy.

For this reason, we should not lose heart, but should seek the nearness to God at every moment, by reinforcing the inner feeling that God is close to us, in our heart and in all Being.

The one who relies on earthly help more than on divine help becomes insensitive to the holy and healing stream. We also set up barriers to healing through our restless conscious mind and subconscious.

We often lack the love for God and thus, the love for our neighbor, which we need in order to attain relief and healing. How often is it impossible for us to forgive—even in our thoughts.

We cannot get rid of our thoughts, our feelings, our mistrust, bitterness, envy, hatred and lust for power because, based on disappointments, we have created all these weaknesses, which we now want to keep.

We think that our fellow people should come to us, speak with us, and apologize. But the one who shows greatness goes to his neighbor and speaks with him, so that many things can be solved. In this way, we give the healing forces the possibility to flow in.

By not wanting to forgive, by preserving our individuality and upholding our grievances, we close ourselves off from receiving the healing forces. If we want to receive healing power from the Spirit of life, then we have to let go of this barrier of mistrust, bitterness, envy, hatred and jealousy, even grievance. We must surrender all this to the Eternal for transformation so that we can be ready to receive the eternal power.

We should recognize and cast off these shackles with which we have bound ourselves and which now hold us captive by surrendering them to the Eternal for transformation. No external walls can limit us as painfully as those of our self-imposed limited consciousness.

Wherever we erect barriers of inner bondage, the spiritual current cannot flow in more strongly. These barriers must fall, so that we can receive the eternal power.

If we learn to become tolerant, to discard our mistrust, our hatred and our domineering nature, we can forgive and master our thoughts and feelings. The healing power of the Inner Physician and Healer flows into us and achieves what human beings cannot.

The inner power can heal any illness. For God, no illness is incurable. The one who surrenders to the eternal law, to the Inner Physician and Healer, is guided correctly and can receive, depending on his alignment, that is, depending on his actualization of the holy laws.

For God nothing is impossible.

Relief and healing are possible in every case, if we just affirm the unlimited healing power of God and trustingly let it become effective in us.

In all our prayer requests, in all our desires and yearnings that we take within to the holy consciousness of God, we should not forget to speak in full awareness, "But Your will be done, O Lord!"

God is there whenever we need help, for He is omnipresent. Let us become aware of the depth of these words: God is here!

God is wherever we are and go. He is just waiting for us to turn our inner being into a receiving station for His holy life, because God unceasingly sends forces upon forces, healing and life energies.

If we have become a receiving station for these life forces, then the divine healing power, His power of grace, is constantly active in us. The more developed this inner receiving station is, the more we receive the divine life. The spirit of our soul is ready and willing at every moment to give to us, even to give of itself. There are countless examples of God manifesting His Love and Wisdom. Many people know about this and have experienced and received His help, His healing power.

We, too, should become a conscious revelation of God by surrendering to the All-power, God, asking for His holy inflow and fulfilling the eternal laws. Then we will come to know and experience and become one with the eternal source.

This I wish with all my heart for all my fellow people!

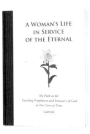

A Woman's Life in Service of the Eternal

My Path as
the Teaching Prophetess
and Emissary of God
at this Turn of Time
Gabriele

In her autobiographical descriptions, Gabriele gives us a lively insight into her development as a human being and her calling to become the prophetess of God—and what it means to bring His Word, His Love and Wisdom to the Earth at this time.

204 pp., HB, ISBN: 978-3-89201-814-8

Gabriele Publishing House – The Word
P.O. Box 2221, Deering, NH 03244, USA
North America: Toll-Free No. 1-844-576-0937
International Orders: +49-9391-504-843
www.Gabriele-Publishing-House.com